Treasure House

Pupil Book 3
Composition

Author: Chris Whitney

William Collins' dream of knowledge for all began with the publication of his first book in 1819. A self-educated mill worker, he not only enriched millions of lives, but also founded a flourishing publishing house. Today, staying true to this spirit, Collins books are packed with inspiration, innovation and practical expertise. They place you at the centre of a world of possibility and give you exactly what you need to explore it.

Collins. Freedom to teach.

Published by Collins
An imprint of HarperCollins*Publishers*
The News Building
1 London Bridge Street
London
SE1 9GF

Browse the complete Collins catalogue at
www.collins.co.uk

© HarperCollins*Publishers* Limited 2015

10 9 8 7 6 5 4 3

ISBN 978-0-00-813352-8

British Library Cataloguing in Publication Data
A Catalogue record for this publication is available from the British Library

Publishing Manager: Tom Guy
Project Managers: Dawn Booth and Kate Ellis
Editor: Jessica Marshall
Cover design and artwork: Amparo Barrera
Internal design concept: Amparo Barrera
Typesetting: Jouve India Private Ltd
Illustrations: Andres Avaray, Jacqui Davis, Adrian Bijloo, Aptara and QBS

Printed in Italy by Grafica Veneta S.p.A.

Acknowledgements

The publishers wish to thank the following for permission to reproduce content. Every effort has been made to trace copyright holders and to obtain their permission for the use of copyright materials. The publishers will gladly receive any information enabling them to rectify any error or omission at the first opportunity.

An extract from *The King In the Forest* by Michael Morpurgo, Hodder Childrens, 1993, pp.5-8; David Higham Associates Limited for an extract from "The One That Got Away" by Jan Mark in *Kingfisher Treasury of Stories for Eight Year Olds*, chosen by Edward and Nancy Blishen, Kingfisher, 1995, p.38. Reproduced by permission of David Higham Associates Limited; and Peters Fraser & Dunlop for an extract from *It's Not Fair* by Bel Mooney, 1989, Octopus Publishing Group, p.7. Reproduced by permission of Peters Fraser & Dunlop (www.petersfraserdunlop.com) on behalf of Bel Mooney.

p. 34 Ensuper/Shutterstock; p. 35 Igor Klimov/Shutterstock; p. 40 gkuna/iStockphoto; p. 41 Robert Harding World Imagery/Getty Images

MIX
Paper from
responsible sources
FSC www.fsc.org **FSC** C007454

FSC™ is a non-profit international organisation established to promote the responsible management of the world's forests. Products carrying the FSC label are independently certified to assure consumers that they come from forests that are managed to meet the social, economic and ecological needs of present and future generations, and other controlled sources.

Find out more about HarperCollins and the environment at
www.harpercollins.co.uk/green

Contents

Planning a story

Read the story plan, and then answer the questions that follow.

This is a plan for writing a story. It is useful to plan a story before you write it to make sure it has a good structure. This type of plan is called a flowchart.

Daedalus and Icarus

Good stories have five parts:
1) The story begins

King Minos of Crete captured a terrible monster called the Minotaur.

King Minos asked Daedalus to make a prison to keep the Minotaur in. The prison was like a maze. It was called a labyrinth.

When Daedalus had finished making the labyrinth, he wanted to leave Crete with his son Icarus.

2) The story builds up to a problem

3) The problem happens

King Minos wouldn't let Daedalus and Icarus leave. He kept them prisoner in a high tower.

4) The characters solve the problem	Daedalus made wings for himself and Icarus, so that they could escape. The wings were made of birds' feathers stuck together with wax.

↓

	Daedalus told Icarus not to fly too high or the sun would melt the wax.

5) The story ends

↓

	Icarus forgot what his father said.

The events in a story decide what type of story it is. A sad death makes this a tragedy.

↓

	He flew too close to the sun and the wings came apart. He fell into the sea and died.

The arrows show how one part of the story leads to the next.

Get started

Discuss these questions with a partner.

1. Why is it useful to plan a story before writing it?

2. How many parts should a good story have? What are they?

3. What is useful about a flowchart for planning a story?

Try these

You do not always have to use a flowchart story plan. Design another way to plan a story. You should think about:

- the different parts that your story will have
- how to show how one part of the story moves to another.

Discuss your ideas with a partner and draw your story-plan design.

Now try these

1. Plan your own story. Copy and complete this flowchart, or fill in your own story-plan design. You can use one of these story titles or invent your own.

- The Birthday Party   • The Lost Pet   • The School Trip

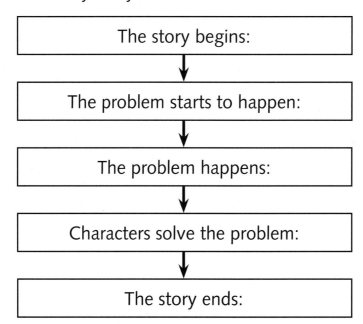

The story begins:

↓

The problem starts to happen:

↓

The problem happens:

↓

Characters solve the problem:

↓

The story ends:

2. Write the opening paragraph of your story. Try to write four or five sentences introducing the setting and the characters.

Story settings

Read the extract from **'The King in the Forest'** by **Michael Morpurgo**, and then answer the questions that follow.

A story setting is the time and place in which the story happens. This author has used descriptive words and phrases to build a picture in the reader's mind.

The same setting can have different atmospheres. Forests can be spooky or peaceful.

Sometimes short lists can give information about a setting. (They often come in sets of three.)

Deep in the forest, there lived a charcoal-burner and his son Tod. They were poor people, but if they worked hard there was just enough food to feed themselves, their cow and their donkey.

Once a month, Tod's father would load up the donkey with charcoal and take it into town to sell it in the market, and so Tod would be left on his own to milk the cow, chop the wood and keep the charcoal ovens burning.

The author describes sights and sounds to bring the setting to life.

The author has carefully chosen the most descriptive words. The horns aren't 'noisy': they're 'echoing'.

One fine morning, with his father gone to town, Tod was out chopping wood when he heard the sound of hunting horns echoing through the forest. The King would be out hunting again as he often was.

As the baying of the hounds came ever closer, Tod looked up from his chopping. Something was moving at the edge of the forest, something white and small.

He put down his axe and ran over to see what it was and there, trembling in the high bracken was a fawn, a white fawn. The hounds and the horns were sounding all about him now, and he could see the huntsman riding through the trees.

Get started

Discuss these questions and complete the tasks with a partner.

1. What setting has the author chosen for this story? (Think about place and time.)
2. What sights does the author describe? Find them and make a list.
3. What sounds does the author describe? Find them and make a list.

Try these

Copy and complete the passage with adjectives of your choice to make it more descriptive.

It was late afternoon and the _____ sun was low in the sky. As she walked through the _____ leaves, she listened to them _____ and _____ under her feet. Sally heard the _____ call of a wood pigeon overhead. She looked up through the _____ leaves still hanging on the tree and spied a nest high above her head. As she bent to gather some leaves, their colours warm and _____, the fading sunlight cast a _____ shadow on the ground.

Now try these

1. How many different story settings can you think of? Try to think of eight different story settings and make a list. For each setting, add a word or two to describe it.

2. Write a short description of a setting. You can write about one of these settings, or use one of your own. Try to use plenty of adjectives and descriptive phrases and include details of the sights and sounds of the place.

   • A busy city

   • A beach in summer time

   • A deserted house at night.

Using dialogue

Read the extract from **'The Talking Bow Tie'** by **Morris Lurie**, and then answer the questions that follow.

Dialogue is useful in stories to move the action forward and to develop characters. It is important to use speech marks to separate the dialogue from the narrative so that everything is nice and clear. To write dialogue properly there are some important rules to learn.

| Narrative | That evening, Mr Baxter brought home a brand-new bow tie. |

| Dialogue | "Oh, very lovely!" said Mrs Baxter, and it was … |

| There are lots of words you can use instead of 'said'. | "I thought I'd wear it tonight," said Mr Baxter. |

Mr and Mrs Baxter were going out to dinner.

So Mr Baxter had a shower, and then he put on a nice clean white shirt (and his underwear and trousers and shoes and socks, too, of course), and then he popped himself in front of the big mirror in the bathroom and put on the brand-new bow tie.

| Characters can talk (and think) to themselves. | "Oh, yes indeed!" he said, giving it a little straighten this way and that. "Very smart!" |

| Put speech marks at the start and end of spoken words. | "Very smart?" said the bow tie. |

"What?" said Mr Baxter.

Put a capital letter at the start of the speech.	"You don't look very smart," said the bow tie. "You look ridiculous."
Start a new line for each new speaker.	"I beg your pardon?" said Mr Baxter.
Punctuate the speech before the closing speech marks.	"You are one of the most ridiculous-looking people I have ever seen," said the bow tie.
How words are said tells the reader a lot about the character. Mr Baxter 'cried' because he was surprised.	"Mary!" cried Mr Baxter, running out of the bathroom. "Mary! This bow tie just spoke to me! It said I looked ridiculous!"

Get started

Discuss these questions with a partner.

1. Why do we need to punctuate speech when we write stories?

2. What is the correct way to punctuate speech? Write a set of rules.

3. How many words can you think of to use instead of 'said'? Make a list of these reporting words.

Try these

Copy and complete these sentences with the correct punctuation.

1. i thought i'd wear it tonight said mr baxter

2. oh very lovely said mrs baxter and it was

3. you don't look very smart said the bow tie

4. you should be ashamed of yourself cried mrs brown

5. it was me he said quietly i stole the biscuits

6. jenny breathed a sigh of relief thank goodness

7. roll up roll up shouted the man in the top hat

8. i will shake her by the hand and say thank you

Now try these

1. Choose eight words from the list of reporting words you made earlier. Write a sentence with dialogue for each word. Pay careful attention to the punctuation. One has been done for you.

   Answer: "Get back over here," yelled the instructor.

2. Write a paragraph where Mr Baxter tells his friend what happened as he put on his new bow tie. Remember the rules of speech punctuation and try to use a variety of reporting words.

Story openings

Read the extracts from '**The One That Got Away**' by **Jan Mark** and '**It's not fair … that I'm little**' by **Bel Mooney**, and then answer the questions that follow.

There are lots of good ways to start a story. You can go straight into the action or some dialogue. You can describe the setting or a character. You can even start with a question for the reader. However you start, the main aim is to make the reader want to read more.

'The One That Got Away' by Jan Mark

Starts with dialogue.

Hints that something will happen 'tomorrow' but doesn't say what.

Introduces a character and their funny thoughts.

"And what have we got to remember to bring tomorrow?" Mrs Cooper asked, at half past three. Malcolm, sitting near the back, wondered why she said "we". She wasn't going to bring anything.

"Something interesting, Mrs Cooper," said everyone, all together.

"And what are we going to do then?"

"Stand up and talk about it, Mrs Cooper."

"So, don't forget. All right. Chairs on tables. Goodbye Class Four."

'It's not fair ... that I'm little' by Bel Mooney

Starts by describing a character.

To gain the reader's interest, get them asking questions. What happened to change Kitty's mind?

Kitty was the smallest in her class. Usually she did not care. She could swim well, and run as fast as most people – well, almost – and once came first in the egg and spoon race on Sports Day. So it did not matter – being small. That was what Kitty thought.

But one day, something happened to make her change her mind.

Get started

Discuss these questions with a partner.

1. How does the first story start? How does the second story start?

2. Which opening do you like best? Why?

3. What is the main aim of a story opening and how have these authors tried to achieve it?

Try these

Here are some different ways you can start a story. Write an opening sentence for each one. One has been done for you.

1. Use dialogue.

Answer: *"How did you two get so dirty?" asked Jake's mother.*

2. Describe a character.

3. Describe the setting.

4. Go straight into the action.

5. Ask a question.

6. Tell the reader something interesting.

Now try these

1. Choose the opening sentence you are happiest with and plan the rest of your story opening. Remember that your main aim is to make the reader want to read more. You can use more than one of the different ways to start a story. You may want to describe a character and a setting, or use dialogue and action. Just make sure that your ideas really grab the reader's attention.

2. Using your ideas, write the story opening you have planned. Remember to make it attention-grabbing. If you have time, you may want to plan the rest of your story. Remember the five parts of a good story: the story begins (you've done that part), the build up to a problem, the problem happens, the characters solve the problem, the story ends. Where will your story go next?

Characters in stories

Read **'The Tortoise and the Hare'** by **Aesop**, and then answer the questions that follow.

Creating characters is an important part of good story writing. There are different ways to show the reader a character. You can describe what they look like, but you can also describe what they say, do, think and feel.

Tortoise and Hare are very different characters.

A description of the character.

The two characters are types of animals that show their different characteristics.

What the character says.

'The Tortoise and the Hare' by Aesop

A long time ago, there lived a Tortoise and a Hare. They got along well until one day, they began to talk about who could move faster.

Hare was a very proud creature and thought he was good at everything. "I'm much quicker than you, slow old Tortoise," he boasted. "I could beat you any day."

Tortoise thought for a while and then said, "I'm sure you could beat me, but shall we settle this by having a race?"

Hare laughed so much, he almost fell over. "A race!" he cried. "You want to race me?"

"You're not frightened you'll lose, are you?" asked Tortoise.

"Me? Lose? Never!" boasted Hare.

The race was set for the next day.

Hare and Tortoise set off from the middle of the wood.

	The winner would be the one that reached the river first. Hare raced off. He was soon out of sight, but Tortoise just plodded on. He didn't look to the right. He didn't look to the left. He didn't stop. He just plodded on and on.
Hares are fast and lively.	
Tortoises are known for being slow.	
	Hare had almost finished the race but he was a little tired. It was a long way. He thought he would stop and rest for a bit in the shade of a large tree. Tortoise was so far behind, Hare wasn't worried. "He'll never catch me," he thought.
What the character thinks.	
	Tortoise was still plodding on and on. Soon, he reached where Hare was resting under the tree. But Hare wasn't just resting – he was sleeping! He didn't see Tortoise pass him. When he woke up, Tortoise had reached the river and won the race!
What the character does.	
What the character feels.	Hare felt very foolish and knew he had lost the race because he had not worked hard enough.

Get started

Discuss these questions with a partner.

1. What do you think about Hare?

2. How do you know about Hare's character?
   Read the text and find evidence for your opinions.

3. What do you think about Tortoise?

4. How do you know about Tortoise's character?
   Read the text and find evidence for your opinions.

Try these

Invent a character of your own and answer these questions about them.

1. What is your character? (Is your character a person, an animal, or something else?)

2. What is your character's name?

3. What adjective best describes your character?

4. What does your character think?

5. What things does your character do?

6. What things does your character say?

Now try these

1. Write a description of your character. Use full sentences and lots of adjectives. Try to include all your ideas so far and any new ones you can think of. Remember to use correct speech punctuation when you write about what they say.

2. Write a short story about the character you have invented. Try to make your character really come alive for the reader. Remember, don't just tell the reader about your character. You can show them your character, too, through what they think, feel, say and do.

Continuing a story

Read the story, and then answer the questions that follow.

This is the beginning of a very long story. It introduces us to some characters, a setting and a situation. But there are lots of questions that still need answering. This is what keeps the story going.

Long ago, King Uther Pendragon and his wife Igraine ruled England.

> Merlin is a mysterious character.

One day, Merlin visited the king. Merlin was a wise man and gave good advice to the king. This time, Merlin told the king that Igraine was going to give birth to a son who was going to be a great man. Merlin also told the king that his son would be in danger from the moment he was born, so he must be hidden away safely.

> What is the king's son in danger from?

A knight called Sir Ector would look after him. The boy was called Arthur. He was brought up by Sir Ector and his wife as their own son.

When Arthur was still quite young, he was taken by Sir Ector to a great tournament. All the lords and knights of Britain were there. Outside the Great Church, they saw a strange sight. There was a huge stone and in the stone was stuck a beautiful sword. On the stone was written:

> Who put the sword in the stone?

Whoever can pull this sword out of the stone is the true King of England.

All the knights tried to pull the sword from the stone, but all failed.

Will all the knights be happy that Arthur is king?

How did the old king die? Is Arthur's mother still alive?

Arthur is still very young and has only just found out who his real father is. Will Arthur be a good king? Is Arthur still in danger?

The next day, a knight called Sir Kay was fighting in the tournament but he'd forgotten his sword. He asked Arthur to go and fetch it for him. Arthur passed the piece of stone and thought it would save time if he took the sword from there instead of going all the way back to Sir Kay's lodgings. He pulled the sword out easily and took it to Sir Kay.

When the knights saw that Arthur had taken the sword from the stone, they were amazed. Sir Ector told Arthur that he was the son of the dead king, Uther Pendragon. Arthur then became King of England.

Get started

Discuss these questions with a partner.

1. What do we know about the story of King Arthur so far?

2. What do we not know? Make a list of things that are not answered in the extract.

3. Who do you think is the most mysterious character, and why do you find them mysterious?

Try these

Think of some answers to these questions. You may wish to discuss them with a partner. There are no right or wrong answers, so be as imaginative and inventive as you like.

1. What was Arthur in danger from when he was a baby?

2. Is Arthur still in danger now?

3. How did Arthur's father die?

4. Is Arthur's mother still alive?

5. Will all the other knights be happy that Arthur is king?

6. Will Arthur be a good king? Does Arthur even want to be king?

Now try these

1. Use your answers to the questions to write the next part of the story. You don't have to answer all of the questions. Choose one or two you find most interesting. Start your part of the story with:

   Arthur then became King of England.

2. Imagine that Merlin hears about what has happened to Arthur. What would he do? Write the next episode in the story, answering the reader's questions about Merlin.

Paragraphs in stories

Read **'Shadow'** by **Chris Whitney**, and then answer the questions that follow.

Writing needs to be organised into paragraphs. When writing fiction, you should start a new paragraph if the story moves to a different time or place, or if a character starts to speak, or for dramatic effect.

Shadow was Tom's faithful sheepdog. He was getting old now, but he was still as friendly as he was that first Christmas many years ago.

> Using paragraphs breaks the writing up into smaller chunks that are easier to read.

It had been a busy Christmas morning. The whole family had opened their presents and there was the wonderful smell of a Christmas dinner wafting through from the kitchen. The noise was slight at first and then grew louder. It was the unmistakeable sound of scratching at the kitchen door.

> A different time

> This is a dramatic moment. A short paragraph slows the reader down, so it makes the moment last longer.

Something or someone was in the back yard and wanting attention.

Tom looked out of the large kitchen window and could just see outside near the bins a sight he would never forget. It was a sheep dog; bony, dirty and obviously in pain.

> A new place

Tom went quickly outside and moved cautiously towards the dog.

A character starts to speak

When a story moves in time, it needs a word or phrase that shows this, such as 'long ago' or 'later that day'.

"Hello" he said. "You look like you could do with some help." He carefully carried the dog inside, and called his dad. The family looked after the dog; brought him back to health and named him Shadow.

That was many years ago now and watching Shadow play with a rubber bone newly unwrapped for Christmas, Tom could hardly remember the dog that arrived that Christmas morning. To this day no-one knows where he came from or how he got there. It still remains a mystery; but it was the best Christmas present ever a boy could receive.

Get started

Discuss these questions with a partner.

1. Why is it important to write stories in paragraphs?

2. What are the different reasons for starting a new paragraph?

Try these

Answer these questions about the story.

1. Which characters are mentioned in paragraph 1?

2. When do the events in paragraph 2 happen?

3. Why is paragraph 3 so short?

4. Where is Tom in paragraph 4?

5. Where is Tom in paragraph 5?

6. What does paragraph 6 begin with?

7. How do we know paragraph 7 has returned to the story's present day?

Now try these

1. Paragraphs are used when the story moves to a different time or place, or if a character starts to speak.
Read the story again and add one more paragraph at the end. Will your paragraph move to another place? Will it happen at a different time? Will you introduce a new person or animal? Will a character start to speak?

2. How would you explain when to start a new paragraph to someone else? In your own words, write some rules for the use of paragraphs in story writing.

Writing a rhyming poem

Read the poem **'Water'** by **John R. Crossland**, and then answer the questions that follow.

Rhyming words are words that sound the same. A rhyme scheme is the pattern of rhyming words at the ends of the lines. The rhyme scheme in this poem is ABAB (because that's the pattern you get if you label the first rhyming sound 'A' and the second rhyming sound 'B'). Poems don't have to rhyme, but lots of them do.

A	Water has no taste at all,
B	Water has no smell;
A	Water's in the waterfall,
B	In pump, and tap, and well.

The rhythm is the beat made by the patterns of syllables. (Syllables are chunks in words. 'Robot' has two – 'Ro-bot'.)

In each verse of this poem, lines 1 and 3 have four beats.

Lines 2 and 4 have three beats.

Water's everywhere about:

Water's in the rain,

In the bath, the pond and out

At sea, it's there again.

Water; comes into my eyes

And down my cheeks in tears,

When Mother cries, "Go back and try

To wash behind those ears."

If you have a word and can't find a rhyme for it, think of another word that means the same (a synonym). In this poem, 'about' could have been 'around', which could have rhymed with "ground".

Get started

Discuss these questions with a partner.

1. What are rhyming words?

2. What is a rhyme scheme?

3. How many pairs of rhyming words can you find in this poem? Make a list.

Try these

Look at the pairs of rhyming words you have found. What other words can you find to rhyme with them? Copy the table and write as many as you can think of for each word.

waterfall	smell	rain	out	eyes	tears

Now try these

1. In this poem, lines 1 and 3 rhyme and lines 2 and 4 rhyme. Write your own four-line poem with the same rhyming pattern as in 'Water'. Call it 'Snow' or 'The Sun'.

2. Some poems have different rhyming patterns. Read these four lines taken from a poem.

- The autumn leaves have now grown old

- And fall in colours brown and gold.

- They fall until there is no more

- A carpet on the forest floor.

Writing a non-rhyming poem

Read the poem **'From my window'** by **Chris Whitney**, and then answer the questions that follow.

The poem has three verses, each describing a sight in spring – flowers, animals, and trees. The poet uses lots of poetic devices to describe spring. Poetic devices are the different ways to use sound and meaning in poetry.

These nouns call up strong images of spring.	**From my window**
	Daffodils and bluebells,
	Crocuses and primroses
This is personification. The flowers are doing something only people do. It is also a metaphor. The flowers aren't actually painting, but it is like they are.	Colour the street,
	Their petals painting the wayside yellow and blue.
	And on the hills
	Lambs stay close beside their mothers
This is an onomatopoeia (a word that sounds like what it describes).	While overhead
	Crows caw-caw as they fly to and fro, back and forth
These two phrases mean the same. This is repetition for effect. It copies the crows repeating their journeys.	

Descriptions need
adjectives.

This is alliteration
(where the same
sound is repeated).

Powerful verbs

To nests high in the tallest trees.

And from the bare branches in those trees
buds burst forth

Revealing new life, new hope

Opening in the warmth of the sun

Heralding Spring.

Get started

Discuss these questions with a partner.

1. What can the poet see from her window in verse 1?

2. What can the poet see from her window in verse 2?

3. What can the poet see from her window in verse 3?

Try these

This poet uses alliteration, onomatopoeia and lots of adjectives.
Read the poem again and copy out the examples you find under
the headings.

Alliteration	Onomatopoeia	Adjectives

Now try these

1. Think about what you may see from a
window in winter. Write short phrases
describing what you see – phrases such
as 'white snow covered fields'. Use lots of
adjectives in your descriptions and try to
include some alliteration.

2. Use the phrases you have written to write a non-
rhyming poem with the title 'From my window' but
based on winter. Or write a poem called 'Through their
window' about someone outside, in winter, looking
in through a window
at a warm, cosy room.
Remember to include lots
of adjectives and see if
you can use any of the
other poetic devices, too:
alliteration, onomatopoeia,
personification, repetition
for effect.

Planning non-fiction

Read the plan for a non-fiction report on sharks and then answer the questions that follow.

It is important to plan non-fiction because the information in the text needs to be organised to make sense. There are lots of different types of non-fiction text to choose from. When you write non-fiction, the first thing you need to decide is what the purpose of your text is, because this will decide what sort of non-fiction text you will write.

The information is grouped into paragraphs and organised with headings, sub-headings and bullet points. Photographs provide extra information.

This non-fiction text is an information report. This is because the aim of this text is to inform the reader about sharks.

Purpose: To inform the reader about sharks.	
Best type of non-fiction for the job: Information report	
Section 1: Introduce reader to subject.	**Heading:** Sharks
Text: Would you like to learn more about this fascinating species? Read on – but beware: sharks can be very dangerous. In this report you will discover many interesting facts about sharks.	
Section 2: Define what a shark is.	**Sub-heading:** What are sharks?
Text: Sharks are marine fish. They live in the sea and are found in almost every ocean of the world. They can be found in both warm and cold waters. They have been around for millions of years. Their ancestors date back to before even dinosaurs appeared.	

Section 3: Describe what sharks eat.	**Sub-heading:** What do sharks eat?
Text: Many people ask about a shark's diet. This depends on the species or type of shark. However, most sharks feed on other fish. They can see well at night and have good eyesight, so catching their prey is never a problem! Some sharks eat crabs and lobsters.	
Section 4: Describe how sharks reproduce.	**Sub-heading:** Do sharks lay eggs?
Text: Different types of sharks reproduce in different ways: • Some lay eggs (up to 100 at a time!). • Others have eggs that hatch inside the female and are then born. • Some sharks give birth to live young. All baby sharks are called pups.	
Section 5: Sum up the report.	**Sub-heading:** Conclusion
Text:	

Sub-headings are useful to tell the reader the topic of each section.

Lists are another way to organise information clearly.

The text does not have a conclusion. What do you think should go here?

This information report is non-chronological (doesn't describe events). So it doesn't need a flowchart plan with arrows.

What is important is organising information into topics. So boxes are very helpful for this.

Get started

Discuss these questions with a partner.

1. Why is it important to plan non-fiction writing?
2. When you write non-fiction, what is the first thing you should decide?
3. What is the purpose of this non-fiction information text?

Try these

Answer these questions about the report on sharks.

1. What information is included in this report about sharks?
2. How is the information in this report organised?
3. How does the reader know what each section will be about?
4. What is the purpose of a conclusion?
5. What should be included in this conclusion? Write some notes.

Now try these

1. Think of a creature that you would like to write a non-fiction report about. After introducing your creature, what facts about it will you include in your report? How will you label the sub-headings? Copy and complete the planning table with information about the creature you have chosen.

Section	Content	Sub-heading
Section 1		
Section 2		
Section 3		

2. Using the information in the planning table, write your own non-fiction report about your chosen creature. This time add an introduction and a conclusion, summing up your report. You could add illustrations and diagrams.

Writing an information text

Read the information text, and then answer the questions that follow.

The text below shows you one way to write an information text. There's a main heading, sub-headings, pictures, and a list to help you find the information.

The aim of this non-fiction report is to inform the reader about sending messages in the past and present.

The information has been organised into sections according to topic. Each section has a sub-heading that shows what that section is about.

The author uses technical language and formal sentence structure to inform the reader clearly and accurately.

Sending messages

When our parents and grandparents were children, most messages were sent by post or by phone. People sent letters or, for special occasions, sent cards. All telephone calls had to be sent along wires.

Today, we can still send letters and cards, and many people still have telephones in their homes, but we also have other ways to communicate.

Mobile phones

These are much smaller and lighter than home telephones. They easily fit into a pocket or bag. Really, they are small computers and can be used for many things. These uses include making calls, sending text messages, taking and sending photos or short videos, playing games or finding information.

Computers

At home, if we have a computer, we can send email messages to other computers. This is very quick and easy, and messages usually arrive almost immediately. Computers also let us have access to the Internet.

The Internet lets computers all over the world 'talk to one another'. This means we can get all different sorts of information through our computers. We can:

The author has used a bullet point list because it is the clearest way to present the facts.

- type and send email messages to other computers
- video call our friends
- buy things from online shops
- send photos and videos
- collect information about nearly anything we need to know about.

Get started

Discuss these questions with a partner.

1. What is the purpose of a non-fiction report?

2. What is the aim of this non-fiction report?

Try these

Answer these questions about the text.

1. How has the author organised the information?

2. Why has the author included the first section, 'Sending messages'?

3. What information does the second section give the reader?

4. What information does the third section give the reader?

5. Why does the author use a bullet point list in the 'Computers' section?

6. Find three examples of technical language used in the information text.

Now try these

1. Think of a topic that interests you. Answer these questions as you think about writing your own information text.

   • What is your topic?

   • What is the aim of your information text?

   • How are you going to organise the information?

   • What will be the titles of any sub-headings you use?

   • What technical language do you need to include?

   • How will you end your information text?

2. Using your answers from the previous section, write your own information text about your topic. Make sure you have an introduction and sub-headings and include a bullet point list.

Writing instructions

Read the information text, and then answer the questions that follow.

A set of instructions is a non-fiction text that explains to the reader how to do something. There are lots of types of instructions such as directions, recipes, how to put furniture together, or what to do if there is a fire. Because instructions tell the reader what to do, they always use lots of imperative (bossy) verbs like **walk**, **mix** or **throw**.

All instructions should state their aim at the start.

Sub-headings help to organise the information.

Good instructions include a list of what's needed.

Snakes and ladders

Object of the game

The object of the game is to get to the last square before the other players.

Number of players

The game is best played with 2–4 players.

Equipment

snakes and ladders board

dice and shaker

counter for each player

Good instructions are clear and to the point. Sentences are short.

Instructions must be written in the order in which they should be carried out. They should take the reader through what they have to do step by step.

Numbering the list emphasises the order.

As well as, or instead of numbers, instructions often use time connectives like 'first', 'next' or 'finally'.

How to play

1. Players take turns to throw the dice.

2. A player must throw a 6 before they can start.

3. If a 6 is thrown, the player gets a second throw.

4. Each player moves their counter the number of squares shown by the number on the dice.

5. If the counter lands on the foot of a ladder, it should be moved up the ladder. But if the counter lands on the head of a snake, it has to slide down the snake.

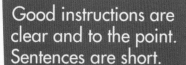

Get started

Discuss these questions with a partner.

1. Have you ever followed a set of instructions?

2. What were the instructions for?

3. How many examples of written instructions can you think of? Write a list.

Try these

1. What is the aim of these instructions?

2. How has the information in these instructions been organised?

3. In what order have the instructions been listed?

4. Instead of numbers, how else might you order instructions?

5. What type of verbs do you need to use to begin each instruction?

6. How many of these verbs can you think of? Write a list.

Now try these

1. You are going to write a set of instructions for making a sandwich. Choose the type of sandwich you would like to make and write a list of equipment and ingredients you would need. Add illustrations to your list if you want to.

2. Now you have thought of what you need to make your sandwich, write out the instructions. Remember to use imperative (bossy) verbs and either numbers or time connectives as you order the instructions.

Paragraphs in non-fiction

Read this information text, and then answer the questions that follow.

A paragraph is a group of sentences that have one theme in common. Most paragraphs have two or more sentences in them but some only have one. It's hard to read a big block of writing, so paragraphs break up the text into easy-to-read sections.

This paragraph only has one sentence.

Paragraphs help to organise the order of information.

Each new paragraph starts on a new line.

The first line of each new paragraph is indented (set in slightly from where the rest of the text starts).

Let's Find Out about Rivers

Rivers have 'ages' just like we do. A river can be 'young', 'middle aged' or 'old'.

The first, or 'young' age, is when the river begins, high up in the hills or mountains. This is known as the source of the river. It tumbles down steep slopes and begins to cut up the rock underneath it.

Young rivers have rocky beds and the water foams and bubbles around the rocks. A young river travels very quickly.

When a river is 'middle aged', it has reached flatter land and is not rushing down steep slopes. The water travels more slowly across a strip of land known as the flood plain. The flood plain is an area on either side of the river that is flooded when water in the river rises over its banks. This can happen after heavy rain or snow.

An 'old' river is the part of the river near the sea. This is known as the mouth of the river, and the water moves slowly over a sandy bed. The mouth of a river is usually very wide.

There are some very famous rivers in the world. The Nile, in Africa, is the world's longest river, stretching over a distance of 6,741 kilometres. The Amazon, in South America, measures 6,440 kilometres and is the world's second longest river. The Yangtze, in China, is the third longest river in the world at 6,380 kilometres.

Get started

Discuss these questions with a partner.

1. What is a paragraph?

2. Why are paragraphs important in non-fiction?

3. How many paragraphs does this information text have?

4. How should paragraphs be set out?

Try these

Read the first sentence in each paragraph. These are called 'topic' sentences. They tell you what the paragraph will be about. Make a list of the topic sentences that start each paragraph in this information text about rivers.

Paragraph 1:

Paragraph 2:

Paragraph 3:

Paragraph 4:

Paragraph 5:

Now try these

1. Choose your favourite sport or hobby. What information do you want the reader to know about it? Plan five paragraphs. Make notes about each paragraph and add the topic sentence.

   Paragraph 1:

   Paragraph 2:

   Paragraph 3:

   Paragraph 4:

   Paragraph 5:

2. Now complete the paragraphs by adding two more sentences under each topic sentence. You have your own information text about your favourite hobby or sport! Well done.

Writing a letter

Read the letter, and then answer the questions that follow.

When you write a letter it is important to think about whom you are writing to and what they will find interesting. You will also want to make sure that you set your letter out correctly.

Write your address in the top right of the page.

Write the date underneath your address.

Write the name of the person you are writing to (with a greeting). Don't forget to add a comma after the name.

18 River Road
New Town
Middleshire
MD2 3SS
Thursday, 12 December 2013

Dear Grandma,

It has hardly stopped raining for at least a week. We have been watching the river, because the water has been rising more and more each day. Then last night, it burst its banks and our road is now flooded.

It's very exciting. We can't get to school. The buses aren't running, and when Dad tried to drive to work his car got stuck and we all had to push him out of the water.

As you may remember, Dad has a rubber dinghy. Old Mrs Fowler had run out of bread and milk. Mum had plenty and Dad let me go with him when he took it to her in the boat. The old lady was very pleased.

Organise your letter into paragraphs to make it easier to read and understand.

The fire engine has just arrived to pump water out of the houses and some soldiers are building a wall with sandbags to hold the water back.

We've taken some photos that. We'll show you when we see you next week.

Love,
Rudy

Don't forget to sign off and write your name at the end.

Get started

Discuss these questions with your partner.

1. Have you ever written any letters to anyone?

2. If you have written a letter, to whom did you write? What did you write about?

3. If you haven't written any letters, to whom would you like to write and why?

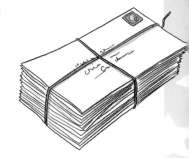

Try these

There are many things to remember when you write a letter. Answer these questions and complete the tasks about writing a letter.

1. Write your address as you would in a letter.
2. Where should you write your address on the letter?
3. What should you write underneath your address?
4. What should you put after the name of the person you are writing to?
5. How should your writing be organised?
6. What should you put at the end of your letter?

Now try these

1. Imagine you are away from home at a friend's house, on holiday, or staying with a grandparent. You are going to write a letter home to your family. What do you want to tell them about your visit or your holiday? Make a list of four things and write two sentences about each. Use the past tense.

2. Use your ideas from the previous section and write the full letter. Set it out like the example letter and make sure you don't forget anything important.

Reviewing and proof reading

Read **'An introduction to Squidge'**, and then answer the questions that follow.

After the first draft of a piece of writing, you should always review your work to check that it has been organised correctly and that the spelling and grammar is correct.

Always check punctuation – capital letters, end of sentence punctuation and especially those tricky apostrophes.

Is the writing organised into paragraphs? Is everything in the right order?

Check the spelling, paying special attention to difficult words.

Pronouns need to agree. Squidge the alien is male. Not all of the pronouns are correct here.

An introduction to Squidge

what is squidges home planet like Squidge the alien comes from the planet Zig. On planet Zig the whether is terrible. On planet Zig the air is hot and poisonus to humans. Planet Zig has no vegetation. The condisions for living would not suit us.

What does Squidge look like? Squidge's appeerance is very different from ours. It has a round body and a square head with three green eyes that flash. Her teeth are sharp for eating meet (as there is no vegetation on Zig) and he spoke with a loud, deep groan.

How did Squidge move? When he walking, he bounced along on a huge spring which had an enormous foot at the end. his full wait is balanced on this he can move very quickly however and jump extremely high

Get started

Discuss these questions with a partner.

1. Why it is important to check your work?

2. What mistakes can you find in 'An introduction to Squidge'?

3. Look back through your work this year. Did you make any mistakes? If you did, correct them.

Try these

There are lots of spelling mistakes in 'An introduction to Squidge'. Copy and complete the table with the spelling mistakes and write the correct spelling next to each one.

Incorrect spelling	Correct spelling

Now try these

Squidge has a friend called Splodge. Read the information about Splodge. It has been written in a hurry and needs the punctuation correcting. Write it out again, this time with the correct punctuation.

1. **Splodge**

   splodge is also an alien he lives near Squidge he has won many bouncing prizes he is blue with a red spring he has three yellow eyes sharp teeth and no nose he likes to eat metal objects

2. Sometimes vocabulary (the words) needs improving. Squidge and Splodge have a new friend. Write a few sentences about this new friend. Read through your work once and change any boring words for more interesting words. Does your writing sound interesting to you? Now read through again and check spelling, punctuation and grammar. Is everything absolutely correct? When you have finished, draw a picture of Squidge's and Splodge's new friend.